VOICES

poems by

Varsha Saraiya-Shah

Finishing Line Press
Georgetown, Kentucky

VOICES

Copyright © 2016 by Varsha Saraiya-Shah
ISBN 978-1-63534-023-5 First Edition
All rights reserved under International and Pan-American Copyright Conventions.
No part of this book may be reproduced in any manner whatsoever without written permission from the publisher, except in the case of brief quotations embodied in critical articles and reviews.

ACKNOWLEDGMENTS

I would like to thank the following journals and anthologies for their publication of individual poems in previous versions:

Convergence, an online journal: "Change Does It", "Dreamscape", "Sunday Affair"

Borderlands: "Voices" and "In Other Words"

Mutabilis Press: "Ars Poetica", "Scaffolds", "Liquid Bond", "Closets Redeemed", "White Coat Rite", "Ironing Curls", "Little Black Dress", "On A Circular Route", "The Day I will Become An Old Woman",

Texas Observer: "For A Man With One Earring"

Between Heaven and Texas, A UT Texas Press book: "There is Nothing Wrong with Us, says The Sky", and "Sky, I Give You My Impression"

The Houston Review of History and Culture: "Muse In The Museum"

Asian Cha: "A Still Life", and "Coming Home"

Squaw Valley Community of Writers' anthology: "This Knowing"

And, a special thanks to all my creative writing teachers and the community of writers in Houston and elsewhere for their continuing support, critique, and encouragement.

Publisher: Leah Maines
Editor: Christen Kincaid
Cover Art: Varsha Saraiya-Shah
Author Photo: Dr. Krishnan Saraiya
Cover Design: Elizabeth Maines

Printed in the USA on acid-free paper.
Order online: www.finishinglinepress.com
              also available on amazon.com

Author inquiries and mail orders:
Finishing Line Press
P. O. Box 1626
Georgetown, Kentucky 40324
U. S. A.

Table of Contents

"Words are uncertain and speak uncertain things.
But speaking this or that,
They speak us."

—*Octavio Paz (translation: Eliot Weinberger)*

CHANGE DOES IT

A long fat potato, sweet and meant
to be eaten, stays idle
for weeks in my fruit bowl.
It grows pig tails and ivory beard
over threads of mustache.
My friend says, *it needs change.*
I pluck all idle limbs fattened
on its sweetness, put them in a glass
with water on window-sill to befriend the sun.
Weeks pass, they continue sprouting
new leaves winding their way around
the mini-blind; my new friends
sing and keep company as I do dishes
drinking the sun-splashed water.
We know what change does, how change rubs on
those who think they're alone or scraping by
or can't make sense of what seems ugly—
it grows new seeds of sweetness,
an assurance.

DREAMSCAPE

In sleep
I am a whole,
a holy one.
See me a grass blade
from any angle
set beside time—

I am a whole without parts,
a holy one.
Sometimes a fruit in the ground,
a free hand holding sky.
Sometimes a breast suckling wind,
a mouth watering earth.

I roam in love to test this and that,
shredding, scrabbling words
to feed alphabets to trees;
hear them speak.
See gods come to shelter in this wholeness.
I marry the grass to my chair,
offer my blood to honey bees, and
become the laughter of whispers
the size of leaf's sighs.

VOICES

> *Forget all harassing noises,*
A voice says.
So I quit the crowd to model in *sari*
draped over a miniskirt.
You see, they call the *bindi* a dot on the forehead.
It is not a tattoo on the heel
nor a ring on the navel or finger.
> *It is my third eye.*
I wake up to walk through the ceiling,
Nibble, sun and suspend my bilingual tongue.
> *A fly inside wall, No more.*
I toss and mousse my hair, shun all that is vanilla.
Let the moon ruffle me once in a blue evening.
In the driveway, I join the stars' gossip—
We telltale and mingle for there is no escape from
What we say and what they hear,
What they speak and what we know.
I bend over fallen notes
sketching hope with broken pencils,
hear the sand rustle, birds bicker.
Even a fading word hisses to be heard.
I flip directories, poring over dictionaries
praise what's unlisted, to behold the undefined.
> *I paint with shadows*, says the voice,
Contour me nude with a meteoric flash,
my eclipsed face in a jubilant profile.
> *Step aside O reason*, my goddess exclaims,
feel my soil-like rawness, she says,
drench me in the monsoon's commune.
> *Go open my spice box for that vociferous cry.*

IN OTHER WORDS

One of the first English textbooks
I remember
stating
a cock means a rooster.

In those old days
only the rich owned *dickeys*—
the *trunk* that moved in a body with wheels
deriding bikers and hawkers alike.

Four letter words existed
only in the realm of a dictionary;
unspeakable meant anything but ordinary.

Fucking is what people in the ghettos did.
Dirty word.
Making love meant babies.
A woman meant not much
on her own,
or when left alone.

ARS POETICA

You trouble me too much.

I agonize your landing—
I dread your departure, always abrupt.

In your disguise I ache
from not quickening that instant.

You stay back, I'm destitute.
Fallen on a leaf a multi-headed beast,

I can't unfold enough
to enfold you in whole.

Promise me—
No one will dare you from me.

To be free, I must flee
from hangout to our hideout,

From bourgeois to bohemian
Be it known

Yours Truly,
You trouble me too much.

SUNDAY AFFAIR

I tell my Brahma today
I'm going to worship sounds
and syllables, my medium
Vedas, don't expect me
to join the discourse or the devotees.

Strip off the bra,
turn off the phone, don a kurta
free of sleeves, skirt without buttons
pull on up in a gathering of gold & fuchsia.

I'm on my train, the screen plugged in
watch me drive, God, no speedometer,
prepare to stop, yes, Ganga—
no pulling chains, no shunting,
no named stations to call out.

The loved ones don't know what work
takes such solitude. I'm not pickling cukes,
or gestating a baby,
it's that thing you know, God, *that work*.

Something to create from room's silence,
sleeping lamps and old windows,
alphabets playing musical chair indoors outdoors
shadows on the wall, this morning unfolding
So beloved to me, yes my Brahma, my affair.

FOR A MAN WITH ONE EARRING

If the hoop belongs to an ear,

Let it be borne, left or right
orientation does not matter.

Let men and women wear brows
pierced for voice,

Let bellies and breasts
be open to voice.

Let studded tongues
rave for the brave,

Kudos to those who adorn both
like the dancers and maharajas,
shepherds and temple-keepers.

THERE IS NOTHING WRONG WITH US... SAYS THE SKY

This noon is glass blue, bottle green
in her fenced surround.
The speaking trees say nothing, but
murmur to the wind, what
The Upanishads tell us:
        Love and Work.
Then, detach from what comes.
Ah, the longing and gathering, fear and fruit.
        Do it and discard.
Each time the itch to belong becomes
noisy and leechy,
Shout out loud.
Your name is not You.
I shout,
crushing the acorns' pointy breasts
under shoes, slashing the side-walk bamboo-
weeds under my bicycle wheels.
The sky laughs and pulls clouds overhead
tipping his hat, nodding—Yes, Yes,
Ride on!

SKY, I GIVE YOU MY IMPRESSION

You are water,
thirsty for something.
I am lost on this city's streets—
A cloud train shunts and lets go
on one side of the highway—
The other side whines about
its brown lawns.
A child watched a tornado
from his binoculars and
wrote a school report earning A+.
You don't know the photo
shot over and over again
by visitors who brag
of where they have been.
A banana peel ripe and slowly
desiccating, turning to dust
looks up to you, and
waits for your word.
Your water has turned me
into free space now
I am neither a woman, nor man.
I am a speckle of time
sexless, fearless, without name, without place;
this being, a new pronoun I call God
made from you and me.

MUSE IN THE MUSEUM

Water seen from the back
as voluptuous as front,
The façade with no pretense,
no form finds force timeless
how we prefer power,
it could be one drop or its entirety.
***

The fountains beat the concrete-
blocks celebrating man's conquering—
Copper coins and silver refraction
the pool offers to man's wish-pond,
without will nothing comes true,
without truth nothing lasts.
***

How the lines man shapes,
shapes forming possibilities
how light becomes color—
Lines indulge inflection of a triangle,
how color is made of light.
***

There is so much life
in the outwardly ordinary.
Her streets and unspoken defeats,
his bravados and unknown alleys,
its hands crossing the forks of alliance.
***

Rufino Tamayo's *The Lovers*
speak with hands—
Face to face soaking up
the canvas, the ceiling,
sky musing over their gaze,
a sea in its blue-blooded sweep.
***

By the window, a willow has scribbled
on glass its cursive signature of light
that staircases the high-rise,
Light shifts full of mind, full of body.
No human will fully decipher
how it loves the willow.

PIANO LESSON

If you can hear it, you'll play it,
so says my piano teacher.
She holds time in her hands, knowing
how to push the keys of each student.
A range of ears and fingers counting notes.

Explains black dots—filled, some vacant, pointing at lines
clung or hovering. Dotted feet and heads
poised to give lessons in time and pitch.
Chords and scales, each with a unique signature.
Major, minor—my hands fumble,
ears toggle keys with eyes,
I wonder:

Am I sharp, am I flat, am I natural?

Start over, each time she coaxes over triads,
or two fingers striking a kiss.
Chords in embrace.
Practice wins, she muses.
Listen, listen.
If you can hear it, you'll play it.

Phrase after phrase, I wait to receive
accord with this foreign language.
A reminder how I waited, nervously
in a line of immigrants. Long ago.
Unable to grasp the nuances of new language:
a range of jargon, rolled rrrrs, irregular phonetics.
Harmony left on a faraway shore.

My new country takes me through capriccios daily,
telling me
The lesson continues.
An octave of a life rarely starts on middle C.

IN THEIR RECTANGULAR WORLD

A pair of window washers swing
in hot embrace of the sun, erratic wind
with buckets of water, soap and brushes.
Ropes secure their bodies,
a clouds' flotilla proffers umbrella, rarely reliable.
Their temporal world on a scaffold
focused on one pane, then another,
their fate in a cradle
that can kill them.
No guard will let them down but their own.
Each stroke promises clarity
trusting the art of their hands' sway,
their own sweat, a climb, descent, a God,
trusting the rescue will arrive
when their knees buckle and palms prickle
on the scaffold's edge
as if trust is their savior, a knowing
that death always lurks at someone's windows.

DAYDREAMING

I watch him from across the intersection
at the bus-stop, sweaty and muscular in a greasy tee-shirt
leaning against the railing
he leers at a *Chica* grooving inside
her i-something, taking pleasure
in her easy curves, rhine-stoned boots.

On the bus, I imagine him indifferent
to passengers' chatter and driver's exchanges
of yes-sir and howdy, how y'all doin.
The *Chica* catches him staring and then savoring
his paper-bagged *cerveza* in a corner seat.

He arrives home hungry and desirous,
aroma of his kitchen greets him first.
His Chicana busy setting the table,
tortillas and *tamalé*, pintos, *pico de gallo*,
shouting at *niños* running around,
Wash hands, Sit down!

He washes away his day in kitchen sink.
At the table, he smothers pintos with salsa,
picks up a tortilla,
asks for Jalapeños, *por favor*, she beams
as he looks up fondly wolfing down her hot *tamalés*.

The bus standstill, sandwiched
between Dodger and a Ranger honking,
the signal blinks red, an ambulance wails.

SCAFFOLDS

He lay frozen darkly pale inside
a warm brightly-lit room, deaf to the eulogy
offered with incense, flowers and fruit.
The morning blustery outside.

Monks' chants rose from a pictorial language,
words invoked familiar spirits.
Sounds made from the body's five winds
deadened inside, mourners mute.

Calligraphic songs wept in diagonal flow
looking for shelter on red rice paper,
bamboo sticks shaped like pyres,
bones ready to restore body with the earth.

Something mystical drifted from him,
through towers of ink, trees & tepees,
geometry unfolding a landscape of loss,
his daughter wept with praise, son mourned "*O Dad!*"

The pictorial transcribed possibilities—
their script grander than the trophies, sculpted
from marble or cast in bronze they brought home
once, he must have embraced lying awake
on his sofa, living room filled with family cheer.

LIQUID BOND

(for Kiki Smith's art exhibit in NY, titled: "Twelve Silvered Glass Water Bottles Arranged in A Row: Representing Urine, Mucus, Tears, Diarrhea, Milk, Saliva, Semen, Vomit, Pus, Sweat, Oil, Blood")

I remember my floor tremble with pain
how the sky crashing with thunder
trades blues with earth,
I thought of us as two hummingbirds
drowning in nectar, one universe
transcending the elemental species.

My tears spoke to you inside the chamber
as we sweated and salivated together.
You even dared urinate in my womb
caving like a pustule breaking my bloody pear—
in its liquid bond you grew.

The mucus you breathed out
left you pure, undisturbed like oil
floating on water you broke loose.

Come, celebrate my milk.
Let us drink
          to the opaque silver of his semen.

CLOSETS REDEEMED

Things we lug for years unaware
how time stores us in belongings
we can't let go from the days' confluence.
The clothes children outgrew,
shoes that lasted a season or two, weary
now released from crowded back racks.
Songs that lulled and buoyed around the crib—
Old McDonald's Farm and Mother Goose's
whacky tricks once ruled motherhood's queendom.
That unworn bundle of diapers
ought to part.
The yellow radio still recites jingles, crisp
like morning glories on a lawn
but faded and distant like the dawn
when I meted out a piece of my youth.
Little doctor's kit, still fit
for my toddler's fat fingers I can't let go yet.
He used to take my pulse
gingerly jabbing a shot in my shoulder
planting his pouty face into my breast.
On the driveway, spring bugs in tandem
chase around the Red Riding hood,
missing pieces of jumbled puzzles—
So many satellites, each with an orbit of its own.
Ah, it's fun playing the redeemer.

WHITE COAT RITE

Orange clouds somersault
into a blue-white twilight sheet.
Tidal laughter cracks open the shore,
      its white noise dancing about
the indolent palms fanning their airy hands.
Moon at her zenith—
light and water hold each other tightly,
the horizon a dark strip of day's film.
Frothy water fringed over rippling hills
the seagulls climb in unison.

In their noisy parley
I remember the mid-day shuffle
of white coats, the initiation inside auditorium.
Scores of angels ready to take off
holding Hippocrates in their coat pockets,
in the gentle tap of their marching steps,
in the dazzling sleeves each a pair of promising wings.
"First Do No Harm,"
my little girl, now freshman, avows
striding resolutely into the tide of healers.

The waves frolic,
white shudder
laughing, transiting,
flapping coats riding on lights' sail.

IRONING CURLS

That evening the three of us combed our hair
grooving between generations
chic and the classic.

You two ironed your curls,
            the electric wand teasing tangles
from silk to a straightened hay sheath.
We giggled, watching it return to a cranky mass.

The reverie of being thirteen—
in swerving braids, black jasmine helixes
I led the girls' soirée
kicked off with a sandalwood dab under lobes,
rosewater splashes all over.
Saris our confetti wrapped below navel—
            Our indulgence rattled uncles' world
that accepted only the prudent.

We rehearsed in velvet black
            our matchmaking aunts forbade
gossiping on porch about destined mates,
faulty stars and the holy colors—red and white.
            Black meant mourning, not wedding,
they would say, pick an auspicious moment,
and enfold your fate.
One told us a story of an astrologer
            whose wife died on their wedding night,
cursing karma and his future even he couldn't foretell.

As you two shunned dresses
custom-defined, tossing what made no statement,
we laughed and tumbled in sashes and slips,
            bare shoulders all evening,
our arms autumn's new gold, glowing
            thighs not shy about the slits.

LITTLE BLACK DRESS

She finds a woven evening of raw silk
pondering over crêpe de chine, taffeta and chiffon—
the small scooped neck seamed to a half-moon back.
Perfect curves darned to a maiden hour-glass
carved from black marble descending
firm, flowing knees.

Bosom tucked inside dainty waist,
trimmed shoulders hold up
postured for the bolero, the back drop
just deep enough to swallow
body's light into a becoming night.

Tiny roses fashioned in satin,
their embroidered eyes hold heat
the three-way mirror carries—
queries that transcend skin folds, shapes
the motherhood defies, twisting answers
to archetype standards: how long must they fit
her body and its contrived images?

A STILL LIFE

(after an installation by Dinh Q. Lê, Crossing The Farther Shore,
at Rice Gallery, Houston, TX)

    I arrived at the port of angels with a trousseau
of silk saris and blouses, a rolling pin
and round board just like mother's to make rotis, containers
of spices like asafetida and fenugreek, home-ground
cumin-coriander I may not find in my new homeland.

    I arrived with twenty-two years packed
in each cell of my body imprinted
with Diwali, holi, and many more festivals,
monsoon at the center.

    Years later, my home has little to do with the old
carefully stored in air-tight containers
in closets. Rose attar replaced with lavender
and incense with none. Jasmine and honeysuckle
still two best friends, east and west overlapping the shores.

    I re-read letters from the far away land
as if nostalgia needs a secure home
stamped *par avion* fading,
when calls and e-mails or Skype don't suffice
or stop me from jetting into skies, and I fly

to touch people in photos once young
    I may never see again, I fly
to catch light of the eyes that wrote, they may
    never write again.

      Mumma shelling winter's pea-pods, Pappa trimming
jasmine gone wild after rains, each outgrown
their frames, sepia shadows,
the red swing on verandah
a still life.

ON A CIRCULAR ROUTE

Little has changed at this bus terminus.
An omelet vendor still waits on transiting fares.
Rows of eggs on his stall neatly arranged like pyramids.
He fries them with onions and chilies on a smoldering skillet.
A few feet away a bull strays, peeing against the depot-wall,
dust kicked with his hooves clouds passengers
shuffling without complaint.
A bull has its right in this democracy.

The route circles the old walled city of Ahmedabad
and her moods; people, dark and light.
Riders old and new to the city's oddities
rarely revolt at sudden jolts and traffic halts,
leaving pollution, zoning, the weather up to destiny.
It's the way of living.

I inhale this spectrum: the mélange of passengers—
brightly clothed bumpkins, urban commuters debating
last year's riots, political parties and the cost of onions.
You grab a seat that cares nothing about class or the caste.
As if saying, Exhale, each time you find or discard
the experience you didn't choose.

A cop still dresses from bottom to top in British-Raj khaki.
A college gal in cut-offs flirts with a pal in Polo,
a turbaned elder keeps deferential gap, wary
not to brush against my thigh as the bus turns, almost falling
over my shoulder, covertly eyeing my non-resident style.

The bus conductor makes my favorite click-punch music
each time he cuts a ticket from his box-like book with metal covers—
not a beat changed, pressing it down in my palm,
jingling the change and ticketing just the way he did years ago
when I used to board from here to my college campus
returning via bus number 60
day after day after day.
A commute that felt like chanting
Om..Om...Om....in a circular rhythm.

THE DAY I WILL BECOME AN OLD WOMAN

Grounds where I grew up will seem
like an aeroplane, the thought of migrating, real.

Nothing would die now, if it had significance.
Even the mosquito I hated in monsoon
trapped in my uniform pinafore,
the menses a nuisance—dead blood
matched its maroon color, laundry's blessing.
The monotony of pain gone with the menopause
would bury itself without body.

Remembrance will be a thing of dream.
Its quotidian world lived out—
Fashions outlived, loves in-grown or re-placed,
Everything de-numbered, except some songs
multiplying still in the making and coming
when I'll be taking out the trash,
whipping out a curry,
or, matching up the scarf with the blouse
just before dance,
the drummer tightening the *tabla*-skin.

WHAT I TAKE WITH ME

The finale of a TV interview late last night:

> *"If you were allowed to take only one thing with you,*
> *what would you?"*
> *"My son,"* the celebrity said, unblinking.

I share this with my son on our way to airport
stuck in a traffic jam.   He chimes in:

> *"I wonder what I would take with me..*
> *My violin, I guess..."*

We hug and hover by the drop-off curb.
He bows, backpack on a shoulder, violin reposed;
I touch his head, a blessing before parting.

He dashes to the terminal without looking back.
I cling to the steering,

the sight of my son being swallowed
by two giant doors sliding back and forth,

traffic cop cries out with loud gestures:
Lady, Keep moving.. keep moving..

that drowns my humming of
Ode to Joy my son had practiced till dawn.

COMING HOME

All flights to Ahmedabad cancelled.
An Agent, apologetic, hands me a taxi voucher
cautioning about communal riots, entire
walled city under curfew, ruffians looting
outrunning police on guard.
Sleep-deprived, my mind half a day behind.

A cabbie waves my number on a placard.
Doors wide open for inspection.
He nods when I greet with *Kem Chho!*
*NRI? he asks.
I nod, he steps aside.
Brown skin doesn't make me a kin now.
I take a peek—

Paisley fabric, seats faded from tropical sun—
          my aunt's balcony sofas.
A dashboard sanctuary, good omen.
Tiny statue of *Sai Bab*a, in framed filigree, a wood rosary.
Faint fragrance of sandalwood, *Jasood* flowers—
          my papa's little *pooja* room.
Ganesh the god, obstacle remover, welcomes me
          with squinting eyes and ample head—
Good to go ahead.

He peels away from the curb, unbelted riding high
on *Gutkha*, savoring his fix non-stop.
Will he avoid Jamalpur Darwaza,
the gate notorious for violence that terrified me most
in my teen years when riots went rampant?

I avoid any talk of coming home
that divides us further,
I ruminate on summer-
vacations long ago riding the local train
from Ahmedabad to Baroda, numerous stops
for local yummies and season's berries.
Now dreading the piles of wreckage at
train station not far from papa's.

Cab's windows rattle, hot cross-wind
activating fans on each side on and off, loud
filmy songs with a static on the radio lulling
my midnight body in a home countless miles away.

*NRI stands for Non-Resident Indian

THIS KNOWING

I have met you and you and you
but can't tell Ponderosa from Lodge Pole.
Let me climb here, turn there through our names,
their inflections and the way each face hands out promises.
I know there is a lift for everyone—
Each who dares to go, rise and fall
flutter and soar and in the steadying frenzy
of nothingness you may wander
wondering what these aspens have to say—
Each shakes and snaps fingers with cheeks
nodding head to ear, toes entwined in music.
Yet each knows to sing only in its own beat
when the wind conducts.
The houses on the hill watch the sun
brushing the trees on the slope deep purple.
When the dark sweeps and silence lifts something beyond—
You tiptoe – still asking,
Have we met yet?

Born and raised in Gujarat, India, **Varsha Saraiya-Shah** has lived in Houston most of her life. She has studied poetry through workshops and conferences in Houston, New York's Sarah Lawrence College, Squaw Valley Community of Writers–California, Reed College–Oregon, and San Miguel De Allende–Mexico.

She was a poet-in-residence at Noepe Literary Center, Martha's Vineyard, MA in October, 2015. She currently serves on the board of Mutabilis Press.

Her work is inspired and informed by contemporary poetry, travels, hikes, music, dancing, gardening, bicycling, human relationships as well as nature and an untiring eye for the small wonders of life.

.

www.ingramcontent.com/pod-product-compliance
Lightning Source LLC
LaVergne TN
LVHW021123080426
835510LV00021B/3298